ECLECTIC EDUCATIONAL SERIES.

McGUFFEY'S

ECLECTIC PRIMER.

REVISED EDITION.

NEW YORK ∴ CINCINNATI ∴ CHICAGO

VAN NOSTRAND REINHOLD COMPANY

PREFACE.

The flattering success of McGuffey's Revised Readers, and the inquiry for more primary reading matter to be used in the first year of school work, have induced the Publishers to prepare a REVISED PRIMER, which may be used to precede the First Reader of any well arranged series.

The method pursued is the same as that in McGuffey's Revised Readers, and the greatest possible care has been taken to insure a gradation suited to the youngest children. Only about six new words are to be mastered in each lesson. These new words and the new elementary sounds are always to be found in the vocabulary of the lesson in which they are first used.

The plan of the book enables the teacher to pursue the Phonic Method, the Word Method, the Alphabet Method, or any combination of these methods.

Illustrations of the best character have been freely supplied, and the skilled teacher will be able to use them to great advantage.

The script exercises throughout the book and the slate exercises at the close, have been specially written and carefully engraved for this Primer; they may be used to teach the reading of script, and as exercises in learning to write.

In the full confidence that the public will appreciate a cheap and attractive Primer of this character, the Publishers have spared no expense to make this book equal, in type, paper, and illustrations, to any that have been issued from their Press.

(iii)

THE ALPHABET.

A B C D

E F G H

I J K L

M N O P

Q R S T

U V W X

Y Z

THE ALPHABET.

---

a   b   c   d

e   f   g   h

i   j   k   l

m   n   o   p

q   r   s   t

u   v   w   x

y   z

McGUFFEY'S ECLECTIC PRIMER

LESSON 1

a   ănd   eăt   răt

ă   e   d   n   r   t

a rat   a cat

A cat   A rat

A cat and a rat.

A rat and a cat.

(7)

LESSON II.

ăt the răn hăṣ

Ănn

h th ṣ

The cat   the rat

The cat has a rat.

The rat ran at Ann.

Ann has a cat.

The cat ran at the rat.

LESSON III.

Năt   hăt   făn   căn

f

a fan   a hat

Ann and Nat.
Ann has a fan.
Nat has a hat.
Ann can fan Nat.

LESSON IV.

mănă căp

lăd săt

l m p s

a cap the lad

A man and a lad.
The man sat; the lad ran.
The man has a hat.
The lad has a cap.

LESSON V.—REVIEW.

The cat and the rat ran.

Ann sat, and Nat ran.

A rat ran at Nat.

Can Ann fan the lad?

The man and the lad.

The man has a cap.

The lad has a fan.

Has Ann a hat?

Ann has a hat and a fan.

---

a at rat sat

can cap lad and

The cat ran. Ann ran.

The man has a hat.

LESSON VI.

dŏḡ   Răb

făt   Năt's

ŏ   b   ḡ

Nat's cap   a fat dog

Has the lad a dog?

The lad has a fat dog.

The dog has Nat's cap.

Nat and Rab ran.

Rab ran at a cat.

LESSON VII.

sēe   sēeṣ   frŏḡ

ŏn   lŏḡ

ē

a log   the frog

See the frog on a log.

Rab sees the frog.

Can the frog see Rab?

The frog can see the dog.

Rab ran at the frog.

LESSON VIII.

ĭt	stănd	Ann's
ĭş	lămp	măt
	ĭ	

a mat   the stand

See the lamp! It is on a mat.
The mat is on the stand.
The lamp is Nat's, and the mat
is Ann's.

LESSON IX.

Tŏm	năḡ	nŏt
hĭm	eătch	hē
hĭṣ	͵ch	

See the nag! It is Tom's nag.

Can Tom catch his nag?

He can not catch him.

The dog ran at the nag, and the
nag ran.

LESSON X.—REVIEW.

Tom's nag is fat; his dog is not
　fat.　Nat is on Tom's nag.

Nat's dog, Rab, can not catch
　the rat.

See the frog on the log.

A lad sees the frog.

The lad can not catch it.

A cat is on the mat; the cat
　sees a rat.

Ann's fan is on the stand.

The man has a lamp.

A dog ran at the man.

Ann sat on a log.

————————

Tom sees Nat's dog.

A fat frog is on the log.

Can not Rab catch it?

LESSON XI

nĕst	thĭs	ĕḡḡs̩	shē
ĭn	ḡĕt		
bŏx	hĕn		

ĕ   x   sh

the box   a nest

This is a fat hen. The hen has a nest in the box.

She has eggs in the nest.

A cat sees the nest, and can get the eggs.

LESSON XII.

ōld

rŭn

fŏx

ō   ŭ

Can this old fox catch the hen?
The fox can catch the hen, and
get the eggs in the nest.
Run, Rab, and catch the fox.

This nest has eggs in it.

LESSON XIII.

pŏnd   dŭcks   thĕm   fēed

Nĕll

I

bȳ

wĭll

i   ȳ   ck   w

Nell is by the pond.

I see ducks on the pond.

Nell sees the ducks, and will feed them.

She can not get the ducks.

LESSON XIV.

hōldṣ tọ

blĭnd Mā'rȳ̆

hănd kīnd

ā ọ k y̆

This old man can not see. He is blind.

Mary holds him by the hand.

She is kind to the old blind man.

LESSON XV.—REVIEW.

I see ducks on the pond; Tom will feed them.

Tom is blind; he holds a box in his hand.

Nell is kind to him.

This old hen has a nest.

Mary will run and get the eggs.

LESSON XVI.

Sūe   dŏll   drĕss   new   hẽr

lĕt

ẽ

ū

ew

Sue has a doll.

It has a new dress.

She will let Ann hold the doll in her hands, and Ann will fan it.

Sue is kind to Ann.

LESSON XVII.

thêre

five   bîrd

trēe   rŏb   dọ

ê   ĩ   v

A bird is in the tree. It has a nest there.

The nest has five eggs in it.

Do not rob the nest.

Will the bird let the cat get her five eggs?

LESSON XVIII.

cāġe

pĕt

sĭng

lĭveṣ

sō

lŏveṣ

ȯ

ġ

ng

This is a pet bird.

It lives in a new cage.

It will stand on Sue's hand, and sing.

Sue loves her pet bird.

So do I love it.

LESSON XIX.

äre　　you　　yĕs　　fȧst　　too
līke　　boyṣ　　ŏf (ŏv)　　plāy

à　　ä　　y　　oy

Do you see the boys at play?

Yes, I see them; there are five
of them.

Tom is too fat to run fast.
Nat can catch him.

I like to see boys play.

LESSON XX.—REVIEW.

Sue has a doll and a pet bird.

Her doll has a new dress and a cap.

Sue loves Mary, and will let her hold the doll.

The pet bird lives in a cage. Sue and Mary will stand by the cage, and the bird will sing.

There are birds in the tree by the pond. Can you see them?

Yes; there are five of them in a nest.

Tom will not rob a bird's nest. He is too kind to do so.

Nell will feed the ducks.

Sue has a new dress.

LESSON XXI.

what

owl

ăn

wĕll

ey̆e̱ş

nīght

dāy

bŭt

bĭḡ

bĕst

a̱　　ow　　wh

What bird is this?

It is an owl.

What big eyes it has!

Yes, but it can not see well by day.

The owl can see best at night.

Nat Pond has a pet owl.

LESSON XXII.

ḡràss	th̲ey	ėome	ŏff	bärn
shāde	hŏt			
ėowș	our			

ẹ   ou

The day is hot.

The cows are in the shade of the big tree.

They feed on the new grass.

Our cows do not run off.

At night they come to the barn.

LESSON XXIII.

sōon   sŭn

nĕck   sĕt

way   bĕll   one (wŭn)   thêir

ōo

The sun will soon set.

The cows are on their way to the barn.

One old cow has a bell on her neck. She sees our dog, but she will not run.

Our dog is kind to the cows.

LESSON XXIV.

brāve	ĭf	shĭp	bōat
drown	mĕn	rŏck	sāve

The ship has run on a rock.
Five men are on the ship.

If the boat can not get to
them, they will drown.

The boat has brave men in it.
They will save the five men.

LESSON XXV.—REVIEW.

Come, boys, and feed the cows. The sun has set, and they are at the barn.

Sue has a bell on the neck of her pet cat.

One hot day Ann and Nell sat on the grass in the shade of a big tree. They like to rock their dolls, and sing to them.

The brave men in our boat are on their way to the ship. They will save the men in the ship, if they can. They will not let them drown.

What bird has big eyes? The owl. Can an owl see at night? Yes, an owl can see best at night.

LESSON XXVI.

fạll	īçe	skātes	erȳ
wĭth	hăd	stōne	dĭd

ạ   ç   sk

The boys are on the ice with their skates.

There is a stone on the ice. One boy did not see it, and has had a fall.

But he is a brave boy, and will not cry.

LESSON XXVII.

lŏŏk	gō	Jŏhn
hēre	ạll	whēel
mĭll	hăve	round

ŏŏ   j

Look! there are John and Sue by the mill pond.

They like to see the big wheel go round.

They have come to play on the logs and in the boat.

John and Sue will play here all day.

———

The cows like grass.

They stand in the shade.

LESSON XXVIII.

ôr	Jāne	g̃ĭrlṣ	flōor
rōll	sȯme	whĭch	blăck

ô

Here are some girls with skates;
but they are not on the ice.

Their skates roll on the floor.

Which way do you like to
skate,—on the ice, or on the floor?

The girl with the new black
dress is Jane Bell.

LESSON XXIX.

fôr	out	ăṣ	how	trȳ
hôrse	shọuld	hûrt	eärṣ	bē

ọ   nō   û

Look out for the cars!

How fast they come!

No horse can go as fast as the cars.

I will not try to catch them, for I should fall and be hurt.

See the horse look at the cars. Will he not run?

LESSON XXX.—REVIEW.

There is ice on the pond, and the mill wheel can not go round.

The boys are all out on the ice with their skates.

I will let you and Tom try to skate; but do not fall, for you will be hurt.

Look! here come the cars. John and Nat try to skate as fast as the cars go, but they can not. John has had a fall.

The girls are not on the pond; but some of them have skates which roll on the floor.

———

How fast the cars go! Can you see them?

LESSON XXXI.

wõrk   ăx   pīle   Nĕd   thĭnk

wŏod   sạw

härd   eŭt

õ   th   n̲

Ned and John are hard at work.

John has a saw, and Ned has an ax.

They will try to cut all of the wood which you see in the pile.

Do you think they can do this in one day?

LESSON XXXII.

noiṣe　âir　hēar

gŏne　Māy　walk

c͞ool　two

â　oi

Two girls have gone out for
a walk.

It is May, and the air is cool.

They hear the birds sing in
the trees, and they hear the noise
of the frogs in the pond.

They see men at work and
boys at play.

LESSON XXXIII.

pṳll   eärt   g͞oats   Bĕss

ŭp   rīde   hĭll

ṳ

Bess has a cart and two goats.
She likes to ride in her cart.
See how the goats pull!

Bess is so big, I think she
should walk up the hill.

The goats love Bess, for she
feeds them, and is kind to them.

LESSON XXXIV.

blāze   pụt   yĕt   house

fīre

rōof

cạll

rĭng

wē

z

This house is on fire.

Look! the roof is in a blaze.

Run, boys, and ring the bell.

Call some men to put out the fire.

We may yet save the house,
if we work hard.

LESSON XXXV.—REVIEW.

Bess, do you hear a noise?

Yes, Tom; what is it?

It is the mill by our house; logs are cut there.

How do they cut the logs, Tom,—with an ax?

Not with an ax, Bess; it is too hard work; they cut them with a saw.

May we not go and see the mill at work, Tom?

Yes, I think so. The air is cool, and we can walk in the shade. We should go soon, Bess, or the pile of wood will be gone.

Our two goats and the cart are here, Tom; we can ride to the mill. It is not up hill, and the goats can pull us fast.

LESSON XXXVI.

Mĭss   wạnts   woụld   tĕllṣ

rụle

kēep

gōŏd

thăt

ēach

ụ

The girls and boys all love
Miss May; she is so kind to
them.

Miss May tells them there is
a rule that she wants them to
keep. It is, "Do to each one as
you would like each one to do
to you."

This is a good rule, and all boys and girls should keep it.

LESSON XXXVII.

sehōōl   child
chûrch   whĕn
bŏŏks
slātes

What kind of house is this? Do you think it is a schoolhouse, or a church?

It looks like a church, but I think it is a schoolhouse.

I see the boys and girls with their books and slates.

When the bell rings, they will go in.

A good child likes to go to school.

LESSON XXXVIII.

quāil

sēen

mē

ēat

knōw

quĭck

kĭll

ōh

fĩrst

Hĕn′rў

qu

"John! come here. Be quick, and tell me what kind of bird this is."

"Do you not know, Henry?"

"Oh, no! what is it?"

"It is a quail."

"It is the first quail I have seen. Is it good to eat?"

"Yes; but I should not like to kill it."

LESSON XXXIX.

Kāte   dēar

nāme   blūe

bā′bў   nēar

shŭt   crĭb

sĭt

Is not this a dear baby in the crib?

Her name is Kate, and she has big, blue eyes. You can not see her eyes, for they are shut.

Kate is a good baby; but she will cry if she is hurt, or if she is not well.

Bess likes to sit near the baby, and to rock her in the crib.

LESSON XL.—REVIEW.

Henry Black and Ned Bell live near our house. They go to school, and I see them go by each day with their books and slates.

Miss May tells the girls and boys that they should be at the schoolhouse when the bell rings. So Henry walks fast, and is first at school. He is a good boy, and wants to keep the rule of the school.

Ned is not a good boy. I do not think he likes to go to school or to church.

I saw him try to kill a quail with a stone. The quail is too quick a bird for that, and Ned did not hurt it; but I know that a good child would not try to kill a bird.

———

There is a baby at Ned's house. Her name is Kate. Ned is not a good boy; but he loves Kate, and I do not think he would hurt her.

LESSON XLI.

līght	fär	ĭts	hīgh
whêre	sēa	tạll	wẽre

The tall house which you see on that high rock is a lighthouse. At night its light is seen far out at sea, and the men on ships can tell where to go.

If it were not for this, they would run on the rocks.

How would you like to live in a lighthouse?

LESSON XLII.

wrŏng   wọlf   ŭs   mȳ   tŏŏk

shēep   mōre

wạtch   lămbṣ

Let us watch the sheep as they feed on the hills. They like to eat the new grass.

Do you see my two lambs? I had two more; but an old wolf took them one night.

I love my pet lambs. It would be wrong to hurt them.

läugh   snōw   hĕad   fŭn
mouth   māde   pīpe

gh (as f)

The boys have made a big snow man.

They have put a tall hat on his head, and an old pipe in his mouth.

Hear them laugh as they play!

It is good fun for the boys.

They would like to have it snow all day and all night.

LESSON XLIV.

swēets   mēan

plēaṣe   bēe

bŭzz   vīne

cọuld

said (sĕd)

onçe (wŭns)

"Buzz! buzz!" a bee said to Mary.

"What do you mean?" said Mary. "Please tell me once more."

"Buzz! buzz! buzz!" but Mary could not tell its wants.

I think it said, "Please let me get some sweets in this vine."

LESSON XLV.—REVIEW.

One day Nat and I sat on the high hill by the sea, where the tall lighthouse stands. We could look far out, and could see the ships at sea.

As we sat there, we saw a man near by, with some sheep and lambs. The man had a pipe in his mouth. He sat with us, and let the sheep eat the grass.

What fun it is to see lambs play! It made us laugh to see them.

The man said that once, when the sheep and lambs were out in the snow, an old wolf took one of the lambs, and ran off with it.

I think that men should watch

their sheep, so that a wolf can
not catch them.

LESSON XLVI.

while	might	tīme	thĭngş
dȯne	rīght	yọur	hälveş

Work while you work,
  Play while you play;
One thing each time,
  That is the way.

All that you do,
  Do with your might;
Things done by halves,
  Are not done right.

LESSON XLVII.

wĕnt

fĭsh

fĕll

sāfe

ärmş

sprăng   wȧş   thă<u>n</u>k   ḡŏt

One day John went to the
pond to fish. His dog, Watch,
went with him.

John sat on a log for a time,
but did not catch a fish.

As he got up to go, he· fell
off the log.

Watch sprang in to save him.

John put his arms round the

dog's neck, and was soon safe on the log once more.

"Thank you, my brave old dog," said John to Watch.

Jāmeş	àsks	wạrm	town
thĕn	drīveş	been (bĭn)	shōw

James has been to the mill. The day is warm, and he lets his horse stand in the shade.

A girl asks him to show her the way to the town. He tells her the way, and then drives on.

LESSON XLIX.

I'll   she'll   dōn't

pŭss   pûr

păt   fûr

härm   dēeds̩

I love my dear puss,
    Her fur is so warm;
And, if I don't hurt her,
    She'll do me no harm.

I'll pat my dear puss,
    And then she will pur,
And show me her thanks
    For my kind deeds to her.

LESSON L.

now   wrēaths   whọ   quēen

wŏŏdṣ   shăll   erown

It is the first of May The boys and girls have gone to the woods to have a good time. See them at their play.

The girls have wreaths in their hands.

Now they will crown some one

Queen of the May. Who shall it be?

It should be the best girl, and that is Kate.

LESSON LI.

Gŏd   smạll   frŏm
wõrld   mo͞on
shīne   nŭt
lŏng   a gō′

Do you see that tall tree? Long ago it sprang up from a small nut.

Do you know who made it do so?

It was God, my child. God made the world and all things in it. He made the sun to light the day, and the moon to shine at night.

God shows that he loves us by all that he has done for us. Should we not then love him?

LESSON LII.

Lôrd	smīle	joy̧ş	tēar	nīgh
môrn	grīefs	wōȩş	stärş	sāy

When the stars, at set of sun,
   Watch you from on high;
When the light of morn has come,
   Think the Lord is nigh.

All you do, and all you say,
   He can see and hear;
When you work and when you play,
   Think the Lord is near.

All your joys and griefs he knows,
   Sees each smile and tear;
When to him you tell your woes,
   Know the Lord will hear.

SLATE EXERCISES

n u n nun

u r n urn

s u n sun

c o w cow

s a w saw

r i m rim

c a t cat

l a d lad

b o x box

h e n hen

k i d kid

q u o quo

p e n pen

j a r jar

e y e eye

g u n gun

v i z viz

i v y ivy

f a n fan

SCRIPT ALPHABET

A B C D E F G

H I J K L M N

O P Q R S T U

V W X Y Z

a b c d e f g h i

j k l m n o p q

r s t u v w x y z

SCRIPT FIGURES

1 2 3 4 5 6 7 8 9 0